THIS JOURNAL BELONGS TO:

Positive Mind

Grateful Heart

Kind Acts

Great Life

SUN MON TUE WED THU FRI SAT   DATE: ___ / ___ / ___

POSITIVE THOUGHT OF THE DAY
(Write a positive thought to begin your day)

_____

_____

TODAY I'M GRATEFUL FOR

_____

_____

_____

TODAY I SHOWED KINDNESS BY

_____

_____

SOMETHING POSITIVE THAT HAPPENED TODAY
(Write or Draw about it)

SUN   MON   TUE   WED   THU   FRI   SAT   DATE: ___ / ___ / ___

POSITIVE THOUGHT OF THE DAY
(Write a positive thought to begin your day)

_____

_____

TODAY I'M GRATEFUL FOR

_____

_____

_____

TODAY I SHOWED KINDNESS BY

_____

_____

SOMETHING POSITIVE THAT HAPPENED TODAY
(Write or Draw about it)

SUN MON TUE WED THU FRI SAT   DATE: ___ / ___ / ___

POSITIVE THOUGHT OF THE DAY
(Write a positive thought to begin your day)

_____

_____

TODAY I'M GRATEFUL FOR

_____

_____

_____

TODAY I SHOWED KINDNESS BY

_____

_____

SOMETHING POSITIVE THAT HAPPENED TODAY
(Write or Draw about it)

SUN MON TUE WED THU FRI SAT   DATE: ___ / ___ / ___

POSITIVE THOUGHT OF THE DAY
(Write a positive thought to begin your day)

_____

_____

TODAY I'M GRATEFUL FOR

_____

_____

_____

TODAY I SHOWED KINDNESS BY

_____

_____

SOMETHING POSITIVE THAT HAPPENED TODAY
(Write or Draw about it)

POSITIVE THOUGHT OF THE DAY
(Write a positive thought to begin your day)

_____

_____

TODAY I'M GRATEFUL FOR

_____

_____

_____

TODAY I SHOWED KINDNESS BY

_____

_____

SOMETHING POSITIVE
THAT HAPPENED TODAY
(Write or Draw about it)

POSITIVE THOUGHT OF THE DAY
(Write a positive thought to begin your day)

_____

_____

TODAY I'M GRATEFUL FOR

_____

_____

_____

TODAY I SHOWED KINDNESS BY

_____

_____

SOMETHING POSITIVE THAT HAPPENED TODAY
(Write or Draw about it)

SUN MON TUE WED THU FRI SAT   DATE: ___ / ___ / ___

POSITIVE THOUGHT OF THE DAY
(Write a positive thought to begin your day)

_____

_____

TODAY I'M GRATEFUL FOR

_____

_____

_____

TODAY I SHOWED KINDNESS BY

_____

_____

SOMETHING POSITIVE THAT HAPPENED TODAY
(Write or Draw about it)

SUN   MON   TUE   WED   THU   FRI   SAT   DATE: ___ / ___ / ___

POSITIVE THOUGHT OF THE DAY
(Write a positive thought to begin your day)

_____

_____

TODAY I'M GRATEFUL FOR

_____

_____

_____

TODAY I SHOWED KINDNESS BY

_____

_____

SOMETHING POSITIVE THAT HAPPENED TODAY
(Write or Draw about it)

SUN MON TUE WED THU FRI SAT   DATE: ___ / ___ / ___

POSITIVE THOUGHT OF THE DAY
(Write a positive thought to begin your day)

_____

_____

TODAY I'M GRATEFUL FOR

_____

_____

_____

TODAY I SHOWED KINDNESS BY

_____

_____

SOMETHING POSITIVE THAT HAPPENED TODAY
(Write or Draw about it)

POSITIVE THOUGHT OF THE DAY
(Write a positive thought to begin your day)

_____

_____

TODAY I'M GRATEFUL FOR

_____

_____

_____

TODAY I SHOWED KINDNESS BY

_____

_____

SOMETHING POSITIVE THAT HAPPENED TODAY
(Write or Draw about it)

POSITIVITY CHALLENGE

When you have negative thoughts or situations challenge yourself to spin the negative thoughts into positive thoughts and/or find at least one positive in each negative situation.

Negative Thought or Situation: _____

_____

Positive Spin: _____

_____

POSITIVE THOUGHT OF THE DAY
(Write a positive thought to begin your day)

_____

_____

TODAY I'M GRATEFUL FOR

_____

_____

_____

TODAY I SHOWED KINDNESS BY

_____

_____

SOMETHING POSITIVE THAT HAPPENED TODAY
(Write or Draw about it)

SUN MON TUE WED THU FRI SAT   DATE: ___ / ___ / ___

POSITIVE THOUGHT OF THE DAY
(Write a positive thought to begin your day)

_____

_____

TODAY I'M GRATEFUL FOR

_____

_____

_____

TODAY I SHOWED KINDNESS BY

_____

_____

SOMETHING POSITIVE THAT HAPPENED TODAY
(Write or Draw about it)

SUN   MON   TUE   WED   THU   FRI   SAT   DATE: ___ / ___ / ___

POSITIVE THOUGHT OF THE DAY
(Write a positive thought to begin your day)

_____

_____

TODAY I'M GRATEFUL FOR

_____

_____

_____

TODAY I SHOWED KINDNESS BY

_____

_____

SOMETHING POSITIVE THAT HAPPENED TODAY
(Write or Draw about it)

POSITIVE THOUGHT OF THE DAY
(Write a positive thought to begin your day)

_____

_____

TODAY I'M GRATEFUL FOR

_____

_____

_____

TODAY I SHOWED KINDNESS BY

_____

_____

SOMETHING POSITIVE THAT HAPPENED TODAY
(Write or Draw about it)

SUN   MON   TUE   WED   THU   FRI   SAT   DATE: ___ / ___ / ___

POSITIVE THOUGHT OF THE DAY
(Write a positive thought to begin your day)

_____

_____

TODAY I'M GRATEFUL FOR

_____

_____

_____

TODAY I SHOWED KINDNESS BY

_____

_____

SOMETHING POSITIVE THAT HAPPENED TODAY
(Write or Draw about it)

SUN   MON   TUE   WED   THU   FRI   SAT   DATE: ___ / ___ / ___

POSITIVE THOUGHT OF THE DAY
(Write a positive thought to begin your day)

_____

_____

TODAY I'M GRATEFUL FOR

_____

_____

_____

TODAY I SHOWED KINDNESS BY

_____

_____

SOMETHING POSITIVE
THAT HAPPENED TODAY
(Write or Draw about it)

SUN MON TUE WED THU FRI SAT   DATE: ___ / ___ / ___

POSITIVE THOUGHT OF THE DAY
(Write a positive thought to begin your day)

_____

_____

TODAY I'M GRATEFUL FOR

_____

_____

_____

TODAY I SHOWED KINDNESS BY

_____

_____

SOMETHING POSITIVE THAT HAPPENED TODAY
(Write or Draw about it)

SUN MON TUE WED THU FRI SAT   DATE: ___ / ___ / ___

POSITIVE THOUGHT OF THE DAY
(Write a positive thought to begin your day)

_____

_____

TODAY I'M GRATEFUL FOR

_____

_____

_____

TODAY I SHOWED KINDNESS BY

_____

_____

SOMETHING POSITIVE THAT HAPPENED TODAY
(Write or Draw about it)

SUN MON TUE WED THU FRI SAT   DATE: ___ / ___ / ___

POSITIVE THOUGHT OF THE DAY
(Write a positive thought to begin your day)

_____

_____

TODAY I'M GRATEFUL FOR

_____

_____

_____

TODAY I SHOWED KINDNESS BY

_____

_____

SOMETHING POSITIVE
THAT HAPPENED TODAY
(Write or Draw about it)

SUN MON TUE WED THU FRI SAT   DATE: ___ / ___ / ___

POSITIVE THOUGHT OF THE DAY
(Write a positive thought to begin your day)

_____

_____

TODAY I'M GRATEFUL FOR

_____

_____

_____

TODAY I SHOWED KINDNESS BY

_____

_____

SOMETHING POSITIVE THAT HAPPENED TODAY
(Write or Draw about it)

GRATITUDE ACTIVITY

Find a jar and create a fun, colorful label that says Gratitude Jar. Place the label on the front of the jar. For more fun decorate the jar to personalize it even more. Then think of as many things you can that you are grateful for and write them on individual pieces of paper. Put them all in the jar. Make it a habit by adding a few more things you are grateful for each week or each time you think of something you're grateful for. When you are feeling ungrateful get your Gratitude Jar and read through all the things you've written down to remember what you have to be grateful for.

SUN MON TUE WED THU FRI SAT   DATE: ___ / ___ / ___

POSITIVE THOUGHT OF THE DAY
(Write a positive thought to begin your day)

_____

_____

TODAY I'M GRATEFUL FOR

_____

_____

_____

TODAY I SHOWED KINDNESS BY

_____

_____

SOMETHING POSITIVE THAT HAPPENED TODAY
(Write or Draw about it)

SUN MON TUE WED THU FRI SAT   DATE: ___ / ___ / ___

POSITIVE THOUGHT OF THE DAY
(Write a positive thought to begin your day)

_____

_____

TODAY I'M GRATEFUL FOR

_____

_____

_____

TODAY I SHOWED KINDNESS BY

_____

_____

SOMETHING POSITIVE THAT HAPPENED TODAY
(Write or Draw about it)

SUN MON TUE WED THU FRI SAT   DATE: ___ / ___ / ___

POSITIVE THOUGHT OF THE DAY
(Write a positive thought to begin your day)

_____

_____

TODAY I'M GRATEFUL FOR

_____

_____

_____

TODAY I SHOWED KINDNESS BY

_____

_____

SOMETHING POSITIVE THAT HAPPENED TODAY
(Write or Draw about it)

SUN   MON   TUE   WED   THU   FRI   SAT   DATE: ___ / ___ / ___

POSITIVE THOUGHT OF THE DAY
(Write a positive thought to begin your day)

_____

_____

TODAY I'M GRATEFUL FOR

_____

_____

_____

TODAY I SHOWED KINDNESS BY

_____

_____

SOMETHING POSITIVE
THAT HAPPENED TODAY
(Write or Draw about it)

SUN   MON   TUE   WED   THU   FRI   SAT   DATE: ___ / ___ / ___

POSITIVE THOUGHT OF THE DAY
(Write a positive thought to begin your day)

_____

_____

TODAY I'M GRATEFUL FOR

_____

_____

_____

TODAY I SHOWED KINDNESS BY

_____

_____

SOMETHING POSITIVE THAT HAPPENED TODAY
(Write or Draw about it)

SUN MON TUE WED THU FRI SAT   DATE: ___ / ___ / ___

POSITIVE THOUGHT OF THE DAY
(Write a positive thought to begin your day)

_____

_____

TODAY I'M GRATEFUL FOR

_____

_____

_____

TODAY I SHOWED KINDNESS BY

_____

_____

SOMETHING POSITIVE THAT HAPPENED TODAY
(Write or Draw about it)

SUN MON TUE WED THU FRI SAT   DATE: ___ / ___ / ___

POSITIVE THOUGHT OF THE DAY
(Write a positive thought to begin your day)

_____

_____

TODAY I'M GRATEFUL FOR

_____

_____

_____

TODAY I SHOWED KINDNESS BY

_____

_____

SOMETHING POSITIVE THAT HAPPENED TODAY
(Write or Draw about it)

SUN MON TUE WED THU FRI SAT   DATE: ___ / ___ / ___

POSITIVE THOUGHT OF THE DAY
(Write a positive thought to begin your day)

_____

_____

TODAY I'M GRATEFUL FOR

_____

_____

_____

TODAY I SHOWED KINDNESS BY

_____

_____

SOMETHING POSITIVE THAT HAPPENED TODAY
(Write or Draw about it)

SUN MON TUE WED THU FRI SAT   DATE: ___ / ___ / ___

POSITIVE THOUGHT OF THE DAY
(Write a positive thought to begin your day)

_____

_____

TODAY I'M GRATEFUL FOR

_____

_____

_____

TODAY I SHOWED KINDNESS BY

_____

_____

SOMETHING POSITIVE THAT HAPPENED TODAY
(Write or Draw about it)

SUN MON TUE WED THU FRI SAT   DATE: ___ / ___ / ___

POSITIVE THOUGHT OF THE DAY
(Write a positive thought to begin your day)

_____

_____

TODAY I'M GRATEFUL FOR

_____

_____

_____

TODAY I SHOWED KINDNESS BY

_____

_____

SOMETHING POSITIVE THAT HAPPENED TODAY
(Write or Draw about it)

KINDNESS ACTIVITY

Make or buy a gift for someone.

What was the gift? _____

Who was the gift for? _____

POSITIVE THOUGHT OF THE DAY
(Write a positive thought to begin your day)

_____

_____

TODAY I'M GRATEFUL FOR

_____

_____

_____

TODAY I SHOWED KINDNESS BY

_____

_____

SOMETHING POSITIVE THAT HAPPENED TODAY
(Write or Draw about it)

SUN MON TUE WED THU FRI SAT   DATE: ___ / ___ / ___

POSITIVE THOUGHT OF THE DAY
(Write a positive thought to begin your day)

_____

_____

TODAY I'M GRATEFUL FOR

_____

_____

_____

TODAY I SHOWED KINDNESS BY

_____

_____

SOMETHING POSITIVE
THAT HAPPENED TODAY
(Write or Draw about it)

SUN MON TUE WED THU FRI SAT   DATE: ___ / ___ / ___

POSITIVE THOUGHT OF THE DAY
(Write a positive thought to begin your day)

_____

_____

TODAY I'M GRATEFUL FOR

_____

_____

_____

TODAY I SHOWED KINDNESS BY

_____

_____

SOMETHING POSITIVE
THAT HAPPENED TODAY
(Write or Draw about it)

SUN MON TUE WED THU FRI SAT   DATE: ___ / ___ / ___

POSITIVE THOUGHT OF THE DAY
(Write a positive thought to begin your day)

_____

_____

TODAY I'M GRATEFUL FOR

_____

_____

_____

TODAY I SHOWED KINDNESS BY

_____

_____

SOMETHING POSITIVE THAT HAPPENED TODAY
(Write or Draw about it)

SUN   MON   TUE   WED   THU   FRI   SAT   DATE: ___ / ___ / ___

POSITIVE THOUGHT OF THE DAY
(Write a positive thought to begin your day)

_____

_____

TODAY I'M GRATEFUL FOR

_____

_____

_____

TODAY I SHOWED KINDNESS BY

_____

_____

SOMETHING POSITIVE THAT HAPPENED TODAY
(Write or Draw about it)

POSITIVE THOUGHT OF THE DAY
(Write a positive thought to begin your day)

_____

_____

TODAY I'M GRATEFUL FOR

_____

_____

_____

TODAY I SHOWED KINDNESS BY

_____

_____

SOMETHING POSITIVE THAT HAPPENED TODAY
(Write or Draw about it)

SUN MON TUE WED THU FRI SAT   DATE: ___ / ___ / ___

POSITIVE THOUGHT OF THE DAY
(Write a positive thought to begin your day)

_____

_____

TODAY I'M GRATEFUL FOR

_____

_____

_____

TODAY I SHOWED KINDNESS BY

_____

_____

SOMETHING POSITIVE THAT HAPPENED TODAY
(Write or Draw about it)

SUN   MON   TUE   WED   THU   FRI   SAT   DATE: ___ / ___ / ___

POSITIVE THOUGHT OF THE DAY
(Write a positive thought to begin your day)

_____

_____

TODAY I'M GRATEFUL FOR

_____

_____

_____

TODAY I SHOWED KINDNESS BY

_____

_____

SOMETHING POSITIVE THAT HAPPENED TODAY
(Write or Draw about it)

SUN MON TUE WED THU FRI SAT   DATE: ___ / ___ / ___

POSITIVE THOUGHT OF THE DAY
(Write a positive thought to begin your day)

_____

_____

TODAY I'M GRATEFUL FOR

_____

_____

_____

TODAY I SHOWED KINDNESS BY

_____

_____

SOMETHING POSITIVE THAT HAPPENED TODAY
(Write or Draw about it)

SUN MON TUE WED THU FRI SAT   DATE: ___ / ___ / ___

POSITIVE THOUGHT OF THE DAY
(Write a positive thought to begin your day)

_____

_____

TODAY I'M GRATEFUL FOR

_____

_____

_____

TODAY I SHOWED KINDNESS BY

_____

_____

SOMETHING POSITIVE THAT HAPPENED TODAY
(Write or Draw about it)

POSITIVITY ACTIVITY

Go outside and collect several stones. Paint them in fun and colorful patterns. Then write positive words on them. Some examples are: You Matter, Be Brave, You Are Loved, You've Got This, Shine Bright, and Stay Strong. Think of your own positive words and use them as well. When the paint is dry place them in various locations in your neighborhood for others to find.

SUN MON TUE WED THU FRI SAT   DATE: ___ / ___ / ___

POSITIVE THOUGHT OF THE DAY
(Write a positive thought to begin your day)

_____

_____

TODAY I'M GRATEFUL FOR

_____

_____

_____

TODAY I SHOWED KINDNESS BY

_____

_____

SOMETHING POSITIVE THAT HAPPENED TODAY
(Write or Draw about it)

POSITIVE THOUGHT OF THE DAY
(Write a positive thought to begin your day)

_____

_____

TODAY I'M GRATEFUL FOR

_____

_____

_____

TODAY I SHOWED KINDNESS BY

_____

_____

SOMETHING POSITIVE THAT HAPPENED TODAY
(Write or Draw about it)

SUN MON TUE WED THU FRI SAT   DATE: ___ / ___ / ___

POSITIVE THOUGHT OF THE DAY
(Write a positive thought to begin your day)

_____

_____

TODAY I'M GRATEFUL FOR

_____

_____

_____

TODAY I SHOWED KINDNESS BY

_____

_____

SOMETHING POSITIVE
THAT HAPPENED TODAY
(Write or Draw about it)

SUN MON TUE WED THU FRI SAT   DATE: ___ / ___ / ___

POSITIVE THOUGHT OF THE DAY
(Write a positive thought to begin your day)

_____

_____

TODAY I'M GRATEFUL FOR

_____

_____

_____

TODAY I SHOWED KINDNESS BY

_____

_____

SOMETHING POSITIVE THAT HAPPENED TODAY
(Write or Draw about it)

SUN MON TUE WED THU FRI SAT   DATE: ___ / ___ / ___

POSITIVE THOUGHT OF THE DAY
(Write a positive thought to begin your day)

_____

_____

TODAY I'M GRATEFUL FOR

_____

_____

_____

TODAY I SHOWED KINDNESS BY

_____

_____

SOMETHING POSITIVE THAT HAPPENED TODAY
(Write or Draw about it)

POSITIVE THOUGHT OF THE DAY
(Write a positive thought to begin your day)

_____

_____

TODAY I'M GRATEFUL FOR

_____

_____

_____

TODAY I SHOWED KINDNESS BY

_____

_____

SOMETHING POSITIVE THAT HAPPENED TODAY
(Write or Draw about it)

SUN MON TUE WED THU FRI SAT   DATE: ___ / ___ / ___

POSITIVE THOUGHT OF THE DAY
(Write a positive thought to begin your day)

_____

_____

TODAY I'M GRATEFUL FOR

_____

_____

_____

TODAY I SHOWED KINDNESS BY

_____

_____

SOMETHING POSITIVE
THAT HAPPENED TODAY
(Write or Draw about it)

POSITIVE THOUGHT OF THE DAY
(Write a positive thought to begin your day)

_____

_____

TODAY I'M GRATEFUL FOR

_____

_____

_____

TODAY I SHOWED KINDNESS BY

_____

_____

SOMETHING POSITIVE
THAT HAPPENED TODAY
(Write or Draw about it)

SUN   MON   TUE   WED   THU   FRI   SAT   DATE: ___ / ___ / ___

POSITIVE THOUGHT OF THE DAY
(Write a positive thought to begin your day)

_____

_____

TODAY I'M GRATEFUL FOR

_____

_____

_____

TODAY I SHOWED KINDNESS BY

_____

_____

SOMETHING POSITIVE THAT HAPPENED TODAY
(Write or Draw about it)

SUN MON TUE WED THU FRI SAT   DATE: ___ / ___ / ___

POSITIVE THOUGHT OF THE DAY
(Write a positive thought to begin your day)

_____

_____

TODAY I'M GRATEFUL FOR

_____

_____

_____

TODAY I SHOWED KINDNESS BY

_____

_____

SOMETHING POSITIVE THAT HAPPENED TODAY
(Write or Draw about it)

GRATITUDE ACTIVITY

Make a list of people who have done nice things for you. Make Thank You Cards for each person thanking them for what nice things they have done for you. Then either mail them or deliver them in person. Make this activity a habit and do it weekly or monthly.

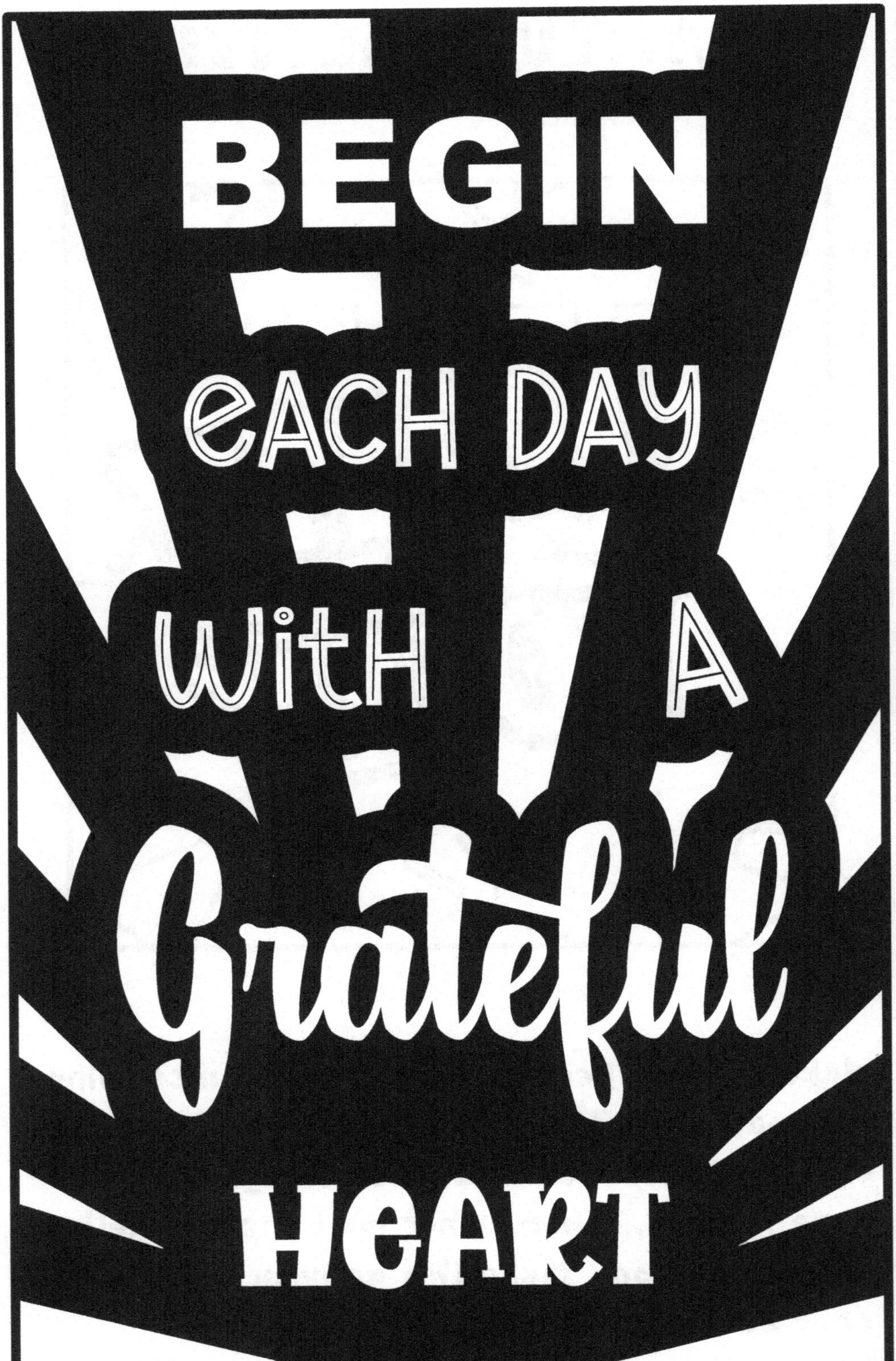
BEGIN
EACH DAY
WITH A
Grateful
HEART

SUN MON TUE WED THU FRI SAT   DATE: ___ / ___ / ___

POSITIVE THOUGHT OF THE DAY
(Write a positive thought to begin your day)

_____

_____

TODAY I'M GRATEFUL FOR

_____

_____

_____

TODAY I SHOWED KINDNESS BY

_____

_____

SOMETHING POSITIVE THAT HAPPENED TODAY
(Write or Draw about it)

SUN MON TUE WED THU FRI SAT   DATE: ___ / ___ / ___

POSITIVE THOUGHT OF THE DAY
(Write a positive thought to begin your day)

_____

_____

TODAY I'M GRATEFUL FOR

_____

_____

_____

TODAY I SHOWED KINDNESS BY

_____

_____

SOMETHING POSITIVE THAT HAPPENED TODAY
(Write or Draw about it)

POSITIVE THOUGHT OF THE DAY
(Write a positive thought to begin your day)

_____

_____

TODAY I'M GRATEFUL FOR

_____

_____

_____

TODAY I SHOWED KINDNESS BY

_____

_____

SOMETHING POSITIVE THAT HAPPENED TODAY
(Write or Draw about it)

SUN MON TUE WED THU FRI SAT   DATE: ___ / ___ / ___

POSITIVE THOUGHT OF THE DAY
(Write a positive thought to begin your day)

_____

_____

TODAY I'M GRATEFUL FOR

_____

_____

_____

TODAY I SHOWED KINDNESS BY

_____

_____

SOMETHING POSITIVE THAT HAPPENED TODAY
(Write or Draw about it)

SUN MON TUE WED THU FRI SAT   DATE: ___ / ___ / ___

POSITIVE THOUGHT OF THE DAY
(Write a positive thought to begin your day)

_____

_____

TODAY I'M GRATEFUL FOR

_____

_____

_____

TODAY I SHOWED KINDNESS BY

_____

_____

SOMETHING POSITIVE THAT HAPPENED TODAY
(Write or Draw about it)

SUN   MON   TUE   WED   THU   FRI   SAT   DATE: ___ / ___ / ___

POSITIVE THOUGHT OF THE DAY
(Write a positive thought to begin your day)

_____

_____

TODAY I'M GRATEFUL FOR

_____

_____

_____

TODAY I SHOWED KINDNESS BY

_____

_____

SOMETHING POSITIVE THAT HAPPENED TODAY
(Write or Draw about it)

SUN MON TUE WED THU FRI SAT   DATE: ___ / ___ / ___

POSITIVE THOUGHT OF THE DAY
(Write a positive thought to begin your day)

_____

_____

TODAY I'M GRATEFUL FOR

_____

_____

_____

TODAY I SHOWED KINDNESS BY

_____

_____

SOMETHING POSITIVE THAT HAPPENED TODAY
(Write or Draw about it)

POSITIVE THOUGHT OF THE DAY
(Write a positive thought to begin your day)

_____

_____

TODAY I'M GRATEFUL FOR

_____

_____

_____

TODAY I SHOWED KINDNESS BY

_____

_____

SOMETHING POSITIVE THAT HAPPENED TODAY
(Write or Draw about it)

SUN MON TUE WED THU FRI SAT   DATE: ___ / ___ / ___

POSITIVE THOUGHT OF THE DAY
(Write a positive thought to begin your day)

_____

_____

TODAY I'M GRATEFUL FOR

_____

_____

_____

TODAY I SHOWED KINDNESS BY

_____

_____

SOMETHING POSITIVE THAT HAPPENED TODAY
(Write or Draw about it)

SUN MON TUE WED THU FRI SAT   DATE: ___ / ___ / ___

POSITIVE THOUGHT OF THE DAY
(Write a positive thought to begin your day)

_____

_____

TODAY I'M GRATEFUL FOR

_____

_____

_____

TODAY I SHOWED KINDNESS BY

_____

_____

SOMETHING POSITIVE THAT HAPPENED TODAY
(Write or Draw about it)

KINDNESS CHALLENGE

Perform five random acts of kindness every week.

POSITIVE THOUGHT OF THE DAY
(Write a positive thought to begin your day)

_____

_____

TODAY I'M GRATEFUL FOR

_____

_____

_____

TODAY I SHOWED KINDNESS BY

_____

_____

SOMETHING POSITIVE
THAT HAPPENED TODAY
(Write or Draw about it)

POSITIVE THOUGHT OF THE DAY
(Write a positive thought to begin your day)

_____

_____

TODAY I'M GRATEFUL FOR

_____

_____

_____

TODAY I SHOWED KINDNESS BY

_____

_____

SOMETHING POSITIVE THAT HAPPENED TODAY
(Write or Draw about it)

SUN MON TUE WED THU FRI SAT   DATE: ___ / ___ / ___

POSITIVE THOUGHT OF THE DAY
(Write a positive thought to begin your day)

_____

_____

TODAY I'M GRATEFUL FOR

_____

_____

_____

TODAY I SHOWED KINDNESS BY

_____

_____

SOMETHING POSITIVE THAT HAPPENED TODAY
(Write or Draw about it)

POSITIVE THOUGHT OF THE DAY
(Write a positive thought to begin your day)

_____

_____

TODAY I'M GRATEFUL FOR

_____

_____

_____

TODAY I SHOWED KINDNESS BY

_____

_____

SOMETHING POSITIVE THAT HAPPENED TODAY
(Write or Draw about it)

SUN MON TUE WED THU FRI SAT   DATE: ___ / ___ / ___

POSITIVE THOUGHT OF THE DAY
(Write a positive thought to begin your day)

_____

_____

TODAY I'M GRATEFUL FOR

_____

_____

_____

TODAY I SHOWED KINDNESS BY

_____

_____

SOMETHING POSITIVE THAT HAPPENED TODAY
(Write or Draw about it)

SUN   MON   TUE   WED   THU   FRI   SAT   DATE: ___ / ___ / ___

POSITIVE THOUGHT OF THE DAY
(Write a positive thought to begin your day)

_____

_____

TODAY I'M GRATEFUL FOR

_____

_____

_____

TODAY I SHOWED KINDNESS BY

_____

_____

SOMETHING POSITIVE THAT HAPPENED TODAY
(Write or Draw about it)

SUN MON TUE WED THU FRI SAT   DATE: ___ / ___ / ___

POSITIVE THOUGHT OF THE DAY
(Write a positive thought to begin your day)

_____

_____

TODAY I'M GRATEFUL FOR

_____

_____

_____

TODAY I SHOWED KINDNESS BY

_____

_____

SOMETHING POSITIVE
THAT HAPPENED TODAY
(Write or Draw about it)

SUN MON TUE WED THU FRI SAT   DATE: ___ / ___ / ___

POSITIVE THOUGHT OF THE DAY
(Write a positive thought to begin your day)

_____

_____

TODAY I'M GRATEFUL FOR

_____

_____

_____

TODAY I SHOWED KINDNESS BY

_____

_____

SOMETHING POSITIVE THAT HAPPENED TODAY
(Write or Draw about it)

SUN   MON   TUE   WED   THU   FRI   SAT   DATE: ___ / ___ / ___

POSITIVE THOUGHT OF THE DAY
(Write a positive thought to begin your day)

_____

_____

TODAY I'M GRATEFUL FOR

_____

_____

_____

TODAY I SHOWED KINDNESS BY

_____

_____

SOMETHING POSITIVE THAT HAPPENED TODAY
(Write or Draw about it)

SUN MON TUE WED THU FRI SAT   DATE: ___ / ___ / ___

POSITIVE THOUGHT OF THE DAY
(Write a positive thought to begin your day)

_____

_____

TODAY I'M GRATEFUL FOR

_____

_____

_____

TODAY I SHOWED KINDNESS BY

_____

_____

SOMETHING POSITIVE THAT HAPPENED TODAY
(Write or Draw about it)

POSITIVITY ACTIVITY

Make and personalize your very own Positivity Box. Then write on pieces of paper anything positive in your life, such as, thoughts, memories, successes, words of encouragement, people, places, things, etc. Put them in your Positivity Box. When you have negative thoughts open your Positivity Box and read all the positive things about your life to push out your negative thoughts.

SUN MON TUE WED THU FRI SAT   DATE: ___ / ___ / ___

POSITIVE THOUGHT OF THE DAY
(Write a positive thought to begin your day)

_____

_____

TODAY I'M GRATEFUL FOR

_____

_____

_____

TODAY I SHOWED KINDNESS BY

_____

_____

SOMETHING POSITIVE THAT HAPPENED TODAY
(Write or Draw about it)

SUN MON TUE WED THU FRI SAT   DATE: ___ / ___ / ___

POSITIVE THOUGHT OF THE DAY
(Write a positive thought to begin your day)

_____

_____

TODAY I'M GRATEFUL FOR

_____

_____

_____

TODAY I SHOWED KINDNESS BY

_____

_____

SOMETHING POSITIVE THAT HAPPENED TODAY
(Write or Draw about it)

SUN MON TUE WED THU FRI SAT   DATE: ___ / ___ / ___

POSITIVE THOUGHT OF THE DAY
(Write a positive thought to begin your day)

_____

_____

TODAY I'M GRATEFUL FOR

_____

_____

_____

TODAY I SHOWED KINDNESS BY

_____

_____

SOMETHING POSITIVE
THAT HAPPENED TODAY
(Write or Draw about it)

SUN MON TUE WED THU FRI SAT   DATE: ___ / ___ / ___

POSITIVE THOUGHT OF THE DAY
(Write a positive thought to begin your day)

_____

_____

TODAY I'M GRATEFUL FOR

_____

_____

_____

TODAY I SHOWED KINDNESS BY

_____

_____

SOMETHING POSITIVE THAT HAPPENED TODAY
(Write or Draw about it)

SUN MON TUE WED THU FRI SAT   DATE: ___ / ___ / ___

POSITIVE THOUGHT OF THE DAY
(Write a positive thought to begin your day)

_____

_____

TODAY I'M GRATEFUL FOR

_____

_____

_____

TODAY I SHOWED KINDNESS BY

_____

_____

SOMETHING POSITIVE THAT HAPPENED TODAY
(Write or Draw about it)

SUN   MON   TUE   WED   THU   FRI   SAT   DATE: ___ / ___ / ___

POSITIVE THOUGHT OF THE DAY
(Write a positive thought to begin your day)

_____

_____

TODAY I'M GRATEFUL FOR

_____

_____

_____

TODAY I SHOWED KINDNESS BY

_____

_____

SOMETHING POSITIVE THAT HAPPENED TODAY
(Write or Draw about it)

SUN MON TUE WED THU FRI SAT   DATE: ___ / ___ / ___

POSITIVE THOUGHT OF THE DAY
(Write a positive thought to begin your day)

_____

_____

TODAY I'M GRATEFUL FOR

_____

_____

_____

TODAY I SHOWED KINDNESS BY

_____

_____

SOMETHING POSITIVE THAT HAPPENED TODAY
(Write or Draw about it)

POSITIVE THOUGHT OF THE DAY
(Write a positive thought to begin your day)

_____

_____

TODAY I'M GRATEFUL FOR

_____

_____

_____

TODAY I SHOWED KINDNESS BY

_____

_____

SOMETHING POSITIVE THAT HAPPENED TODAY
(Write or Draw about it)

SUN   MON   TUE   WED   THU   FRI   SAT   DATE: ___ / ___ / ___

POSITIVE THOUGHT OF THE DAY
(Write a positive thought to begin your day)

_____

_____

TODAY I'M GRATEFUL FOR

_____

_____

_____

TODAY I SHOWED KINDNESS BY

_____

_____

SOMETHING POSITIVE THAT HAPPENED TODAY
(Write or Draw about it)

POSITIVE THOUGHT OF THE DAY
(Write a positive thought to begin your day)

_____

_____

TODAY I'M GRATEFUL FOR

_____

_____

_____

TODAY I SHOWED KINDNESS BY

_____

_____

SOMETHING POSITIVE THAT HAPPENED TODAY
(Write or Draw about it)

GRATITUDE ACTIVITY

Choose someone in your life and write a list of everything about them you're grateful for. Decorate and color the list to make it fun. Give the list to the person you made it for. If you're comfortable read the list to them. Make it a habit and do this regularly. People like feeling appreciated!

SUN MON TUE WED THU FRI SAT   DATE: ___ / ___ / ___

POSITIVE THOUGHT OF THE DAY
(Write a positive thought to begin your day)

_____

_____

TODAY I'M GRATEFUL FOR

_____

_____

_____

TODAY I SHOWED KINDNESS BY

_____

_____

SOMETHING POSITIVE
THAT HAPPENED TODAY
(Write or Draw about it)

SUN MON TUE WED THU FRI SAT   DATE: ___ / ___ / ___

POSITIVE THOUGHT OF THE DAY
(Write a positive thought to begin your day)

_____

_____

TODAY I'M GRATEFUL FOR

_____

_____

_____

TODAY I SHOWED KINDNESS BY

_____

_____

SOMETHING POSITIVE THAT HAPPENED TODAY
(Write or Draw about it)

POSITIVE THOUGHT OF THE DAY
(Write a positive thought to begin your day)

_____

_____

TODAY I'M GRATEFUL FOR

_____

_____

_____

TODAY I SHOWED KINDNESS BY

_____

_____

SOMETHING POSITIVE THAT HAPPENED TODAY
(Write or Draw about it)

SUN MON TUE WED THU FRI SAT   DATE: ___ / ___ / ___

POSITIVE THOUGHT OF THE DAY
(Write a positive thought to begin your day)

_____

_____

TODAY I'M GRATEFUL FOR

_____

_____

_____

TODAY I SHOWED KINDNESS BY

_____

_____

SOMETHING POSITIVE THAT HAPPENED TODAY
(Write or Draw about it)

SUN MON TUE WED THU FRI SAT   DATE: ___ / ___ / ___

POSITIVE THOUGHT OF THE DAY
(Write a positive thought to begin your day)

_____

_____

TODAY I'M GRATEFUL FOR

_____

_____

_____

TODAY I SHOWED KINDNESS BY

_____

_____

SOMETHING POSITIVE THAT HAPPENED TODAY
(Write or Draw about it)

POSITIVE THOUGHT OF THE DAY
(Write a positive thought to begin your day)

_____

_____

TODAY I'M GRATEFUL FOR

_____

_____

_____

TODAY I SHOWED KINDNESS BY

_____

_____

SOMETHING POSITIVE THAT HAPPENED TODAY
(Write or Draw about it)

SUN MON TUE WED THU FRI SAT   DATE: ___ / ___ / ___

POSITIVE THOUGHT OF THE DAY
(Write a positive thought to begin your day)

_____
_____

TODAY I'M GRATEFUL FOR

_____
_____
_____

TODAY I SHOWED KINDNESS BY

_____
_____

SOMETHING POSITIVE THAT HAPPENED TODAY
(Write or Draw about it)

SUN MON TUE WED THU FRI SAT   DATE: ___ / ___ / ___

POSITIVE THOUGHT OF THE DAY
(Write a positive thought to begin your day)

_____

_____

TODAY I'M GRATEFUL FOR

_____

_____

_____

TODAY I SHOWED KINDNESS BY

_____

_____

SOMETHING POSITIVE
THAT HAPPENED TODAY
(Write or Draw about it)

SUN MON TUE WED THU FRI SAT   DATE: ___ / ___ / ___

POSITIVE THOUGHT OF THE DAY
(Write a positive thought to begin your day)

_____

_____

TODAY I'M GRATEFUL FOR

_____

_____

_____

TODAY I SHOWED KINDNESS BY

_____

_____

SOMETHING POSITIVE THAT HAPPENED TODAY
(Write or Draw about it)

SUN MON TUE WED THU FRI SAT   DATE: ___ / ___ / ___

POSITIVE THOUGHT OF THE DAY
(Write a positive thought to begin your day)

_____

_____

TODAY I'M GRATEFUL FOR

_____

_____

_____

TODAY I SHOWED KINDNESS BY

_____

_____

SOMETHING POSITIVE
THAT HAPPENED TODAY
(Write or Draw about it)

KINDNESS ACTIVITY

Help someone in need.

Who did you help?_____

How did you help them? _____

_____

SUN MON TUE WED THU FRI SAT   DATE: ___ / ___ / ___

POSITIVE THOUGHT OF THE DAY
(Write a positive thought to begin your day)

_____

_____

TODAY I'M GRATEFUL FOR

_____

_____

_____

TODAY I SHOWED KINDNESS BY

_____

_____

SOMETHING POSITIVE THAT HAPPENED TODAY
(Write or Draw about it)

SUN MON TUE WED THU FRI SAT   DATE: ___ / ___ / ___

POSITIVE THOUGHT OF THE DAY
(Write a positive thought to begin your day)

_____

_____

TODAY I'M GRATEFUL FOR

_____

_____

_____

TODAY I SHOWED KINDNESS BY

_____

_____

SOMETHING POSITIVE THAT HAPPENED TODAY
(Write or Draw about it)

SUN MON TUE WED THU FRI SAT   DATE: ___ / ___ / ___

POSITIVE THOUGHT OF THE DAY
(Write a positive thought to begin your day)

_____

_____

TODAY I'M GRATEFUL FOR

_____

_____

_____

TODAY I SHOWED KINDNESS BY

_____

_____

SOMETHING POSITIVE THAT HAPPENED TODAY
(Write or Draw about it)

SUN   MON   TUE   WED   THU   FRI   SAT   DATE: ___ / ___ / ___

POSITIVE THOUGHT OF THE DAY
(Write a positive thought to begin your day)

_____

_____

TODAY I'M GRATEFUL FOR

_____

_____

_____

TODAY I SHOWED KINDNESS BY

_____

_____

SOMETHING POSITIVE THAT HAPPENED TODAY
(Write or Draw about it)

SUN MON TUE WED THU FRI SAT   DATE: ___ / ___ / ___

POSITIVE THOUGHT OF THE DAY
(Write a positive thought to begin your day)

_____

_____

TODAY I'M GRATEFUL FOR

_____

_____

_____

TODAY I SHOWED KINDNESS BY

_____

_____

SOMETHING POSITIVE THAT HAPPENED TODAY
(Write or Draw about it)

SUN   MON   TUE   WED   THU   FRI   SAT   DATE: ___ / ___ / ___

POSITIVE THOUGHT OF THE DAY
(Write a positive thought to begin your day)

_____

_____

TODAY I'M GRATEFUL FOR

_____

_____

_____

TODAY I SHOWED KINDNESS BY

_____

_____

SOMETHING POSITIVE THAT HAPPENED TODAY
(Write or Draw about it)

SUN   MON   TUE   WED   THU   FRI   SAT   DATE: ___ / ___ / ___

POSITIVE THOUGHT OF THE DAY
(Write a positive thought to begin your day)

_____

_____

TODAY I'M GRATEFUL FOR

_____

_____

_____

TODAY I SHOWED KINDNESS BY

_____

_____

SOMETHING POSITIVE THAT HAPPENED TODAY
(Write or Draw about it)

SUN MON TUE WED THU FRI SAT   DATE: ___ / ___ / ___

POSITIVE THOUGHT OF THE DAY
(Write a positive thought to begin your day)

_____

_____

TODAY I'M GRATEFUL FOR

_____

_____

_____

TODAY I SHOWED KINDNESS BY

_____

_____

SOMETHING POSITIVE THAT HAPPENED TODAY
(Write or Draw about it)

SUN MON TUE WED THU FRI SAT   DATE: ___ / ___ / ___

POSITIVE THOUGHT OF THE DAY
(Write a positive thought to begin your day)

_____

_____

TODAY I'M GRATEFUL FOR

_____

_____

_____

TODAY I SHOWED KINDNESS BY

_____

_____

SOMETHING POSITIVE THAT HAPPENED TODAY
(Write or Draw about it)

SUN MON TUE WED THU FRI SAT   DATE: ___ / ___ / ___

POSITIVE THOUGHT OF THE DAY
(Write a positive thought to begin your day)

_____

_____

TODAY I'M GRATEFUL FOR

_____

_____

_____

TODAY I SHOWED KINDNESS BY

_____

_____

SOMETHING POSITIVE THAT HAPPENED TODAY
(Write or Draw about it)

KINDNESS ACTIVITY

Say something nice to one or more people by creating a Compliment Card that compliments something about that person or persons. For example, you can write, "You're making a difference," or "I'm proud of you," or "Good job." There are many ways to compliment others. Think of something that is meaningful to that person in particular. Then give them the card. Make it a habit and do this activity weekly or monthly. People like being complimented!

VISIT US AT

www.littlejoypress.com/kindness

FOR FREE EXTRAS

YOUR DOWNLOAD CODE: KINDNESS

FOLLOW US

 @LiTTLeJOYPRESS

 LiTTLe JOY PRESS